Paths and Aspirations of the Enlightened Ones

A book of Buddhist liturgies meant for recitation at the places of Buddhist pilgrimage, at times of the year astrologically connected with the life of Buddha Shakyamuni, at public gatherings where such a rite is required, or as a daily reading practice for interested individuals

Compiled by

The Office of His Holiness the Dalai Lama

Rendered into English at

The Translation Department
Library of Tibetan Works and Archives

First Published in 1981
Second Edition: 2005

ISBN: 81-86470-40-9

Published by the Library of Tibetan Works and Archives, Dharamsala and printed at Indraprastha Press (CBT), 4 Bahadur Shah Zafar Marg, New Delhi-110002

Contents

Publisher's Note

In the spring of 1979 the Library of Tibetan Works and Archives was given the Tibetan manuscript of a collection of contemplative prayers compiled and edited by the Office of His Holiness the Dalai Lama. Entitled *Paths and Aspirations of the Enlightened Ones,* this collection was unique in that it drew all its material from ancient and classical Indian Buddhist works as preserved in Tibetan translation in the *Kanjur* and *Tanjur*, and, in the case of certain verses, in the oral tradition. It was felt that if this text were translated into English, it may fulfil a need in the growing Western Buddhist movement, and therefore Ven. Thepo Tulku and Glenn H. Mullin, two members of the Translation Bureau of the Library of Tibetan Works and Archives, were directed to prepare an English rendition.

However, because the work was structured upon more than a dozen early Indian pieces popular in all major Tibetan traditions today, a number of items within it already existed in English. Four of these have been incorporated without revision in this volume: "A Sutra to the Thirty-Five Buddhas: Confessing a Bodhisattva's Downfalls," translated by Ven. Thubten Zopa Rinphoche, International Mahayanist Institute, Nepal, 1975; "An Aspirational Prayer in Seventy Stanzas" by Aryasura, translated by Ven. Doboom Tulku and Brian Beresford in the text *Aryasura's Aspiration and A Meditation on Compassion,* LTWA; Shantideva's "Dedication", translated by Gelong Jampa Tapkay, or Stephen Batchelor, as chapter ten of *A Guide to the Bodhisattva's Way of Life,* also published by the LTWA; and Prof. Robert Thurman's translation of "The Vow of Universal Goodness" selected from the *Avatamsaka Sutra* (previously unpublished).

In the case of shorter passages of the collection that already existed in English, the translators preferred to rework these, rather than incorporate existing versions, to avoid the problems in recitation caused by too many changes in translation style.

The translators would like to acknowledge the invaluable assistance of Geshey Sonam Rinchen, who clarified all difficult passages and gave much of his precious time to the work.

Of note to students of Tibetan Language, the Tibetan version of this text has now been published by the Office of His Holiness the Dalai Lama, Tekchen Choling, Dharamsala, H.P. India, and is available through the Tibetan Monastery, Bodh Gaya, Bihar, India.

Gyatsho Tsering,
Director,
LTWA, 1981

Addendum to Publisher's Note

This publication was first printed in 1981 under the title *The Sublime Path of the Victorious Ones* and has remained out of print for a long time.

We are happy to bring out this second edition under the new title *Paths and Aspirations of the Enlightened Ones* and hope it will benefit and fulfil the aspirations of many Buddhist practitioners.

Publication Department
LTWA
July, 2005

Compiler's Introduction

Previously in the great places of Buddhist pilgrimage—such as Bodh Gaya, the Diamond Seat of the Heart of Enlightenment where is found the sacred tree under which Shakyamuni manifested full awakening—monks of the Tibetan tradition generally have performed some type of Lama Chopa Rite together with the tantric offering of Tsok. However, these places are frequented by pilgrims holding the views and practices of both Theravadin and Mahayana traditions, as well as by many non-Buddhists. All of these groups have differing attitudes and mental dispositions toward spiritual practice, and the Lama Chöpa Rite and Tsok Offering mentioned above, belonging exclusively to the Mahanuttarayoga division of the secret Buddhist Tantras, are not really appropriate except on special occasions. The same situation was seen to exist for general Buddhist gatherings on holy days, such as those associated with various deeds of Buddha Shakyamuni and other renowned Buddhist masters.

With this thought His Holiness the Dalai Lama instructed his Private Office to draw from the Kanjur (Collection of original Buddhist Sutras, Tantras, etc.) and *Tanjur* (Collection of translated works by later Indian Buddhist masters) and compile a book of Buddhist liturgies (in Tibetan) that would be in accordance with the Sutrayana Tradition, and that could serve as a recitational manual for all pilgrims to the holy places—whether monks or laymen, Mahayana or otherwise, formal Buddhist or not. It was suggested that this book could also be of use at general Buddhist gatherings on holy occasions and also as a daily reading practice for interested individuals.

Thus we began compilation of this work, which is structured and arranged in accordance with the standard meditational stages of taking Refuge, generating the bodhimind, making offerings and praises, recitation of the Buddha Shakyamuni mantra, making requests and requests and aspirational prayers, dedication, etc. This material was then presented to His Holiness for correction and approval.

The compiler and editor would like to acknowledge the assistance of Geshey Palden Drakpa, Librarian at Tibet House, New Delhi, who helped in the search for appropriate prayers from amongst those found in the *Tanjur*.

May any merit of this small Dharma effort cause the precious doctrine of the Enlightened One to be revived and strengthened, and to remain in this world for long, that the living beings belaboured by dissatisfaction, misery and confusion may be refreshed and brought to happiness.

Doboom Tulku
Secretary,
Office of His Holiness the Dalai Lama,
The auspicious Fourth Month of the Iron Bird Year

Paths and Aspirations of the Enlightened Ones

I
The Preliminaries

1. Refuge

To the holy Teachers—both my all-kind root Guru and the entire lineage of Gurus—who in nature are the body, speech, mind, qualities and enlightened activity of the Tathagatas of the ten directions and three times, and who are the source of the eighty thousand categories of the Dharma, and are lords amongst all the exalted Sangha, I turn for refuge. To the Buddha I turn for refuge. To the Dharma I turn for refuge. To the Sangha I turn for refuge. To the Meditational Deities and the deities of their mandalas I turn for refuge. And to the glorious, holy Dharma Protectors, possessors of eyes of wisdom, I turn for refuge. *(3X)*

2. Generating the Bodhimind

To Buddha, Dharma and the Spiritual Community
Until enlightenment I turn for refuge.
By my practice of the six perfections
May Buddhahood be attained for the sake of all. *(3X)*

To the Three Jewels I turn for refuge,
All my negativities I now lay bare,
In the goodness of living beings I rejoice,
The enlightened mind of the Buddha I seize.

To Buddha, Dharma and the Sangha
Until enlightenment I turn for refuge.
In order to fulfil the needs of myself and others
I give birth to the bodhimind.

Having given birth to the sacred bodhimind,
I will invite all beings to a feast of joy.
I will pursue the beautiful ways of enlightenment
And for the benefit of beings will actualize Buddhahood.

(*Repeat these last three verses three times.*)

3. Engendering the four immeasurable aspirations

May all living beings have happiness and its cause;
May all living beings be separated from suffering and its cause;
May they never be separated from that happiness which is beyond suffering;
And may they abide in that equanimity which is without attraction to the near or aversion to the far.[1] *(3X)*

4. Verses of homage

Homage to the perfect Buddha,
Supreme sage amongst teachers,
Who taught dependent arising to be
Ceaseless and birthless.

Not without existence yet not permanent,
Without coming and without going,
Not diverse yet not oneness,
Totally free of all entanglements.[2]

Homage to the spiritual sources of the Sravaka Arhants, Pratyekabuddhas and Buddhas;
The Sravakas, seekers of peace who are led to peace by the knowledge of the foundation;
The Bodhisattvas, who aspire to benefit living beings and to accomplish the needs of the world;

And the Buddhas, masters in possession of omniscient wisdom able to teach all the various ways.

5. Purifying the environment

May the entire face of the earth
Become without thorns or hindrances,
As level as the palm of one's hand
And as smooth as lapiz lazuli.

6. Consecrating the offering materials

May the skies be totally filled
With clouds of the offerings of men and gods,
Offering both real and imagined
Arranged in Samantabhadra's peerless way.

OM NAMO BHAGA-VATE, VAJRA SARA PRAMARDA-NE, TATHAGATAYA ARHATE, SAMYAK SAMBUDDHAYA, TAD YATHA, OM VAJR VAJR MAHA-VAJRA, MAHA TEJA VAJR, MAHA VIDYA VAJRE, MAHA BODHICHITTA VAJRE, MAHAMANDOPA SAMKRAMNA VAJRE, BODHI SARVA KARMA AVARNA VISHODHANO VAJRE SVAHA *(3X)*

7. Calling upon the powers of truth

By the truth of the Three Precious Jewels, the blessings of the perfect collections of merit and wisdom, and the strength of the incomprehensible Dharmadhatu, may these very wishes come true. *(3X)*

II

The Invocation

O Bhagawan, protector of all living beings,
Destroyer of mara and his evil armies,
Perfect knower of all that is,
Pray, together with your retinue, descend.[3]

O Buddha, who for countless aeons practised
Compassion for the infinite beings
And fulfilled your vast prayers,
The time to act has come.

Come forth from your Dharmadhatu palace;
Reveal your magical powers and blessings.
In order to liberate the countless beings,
Come forth with your retinue.

Lord and master of all the Dharmas,
You who have the colour of pure gold
And whose brilliance outshines the sun,
With devotion I invite you to come.

Peaceful and compassionate one
Who abides in discipline and samadhi,
Whose passionless wisdom secs all things
And is of inexhaustible energy;

Lord of peaceful lords, come forth, come forth.
Supreme of Able Ones, omniscient one
With a form like a radiant reflection,
Be moved by my devotion and come forth.

For the sake of the living beings you dwell
In the sacred images now before us;
Pray, then, grant us the health, long life,
Prosperity and all things good.

O Buddha, how auspicious were you to manifest
To prove the power of goodness.
Descend, accept our offerings
And look upon us with compassion.

Thus Gone One, Victorious and Transcendent One,
Come forth; descend to this very place.
Accept these our humble offerings
And abide here in this very place.

Out of compassion for me and the limitless beings
Reveal the might of your magical powers.
O Bhagawan, I pray, abide here
For as long as we propitiate you.

III

Making Offerings[4]

1. Offering the mystical bath

O Conquerors and Transcended Ones, Thus Gone Ones,
Destroyers of the foe Delusion,
Perfectly Awakened Ones whose feet are wisdom itself,
The Gone to Bliss, Knowers of the World,

Guides who tame the uncivilized beings,
Supreme Ones, Teachers of Men and Gods,
O Buddhas and Bhagawans,
I offer you this bath resplendent with all things good.

I visualize a bath house of sweet fragrance
With a crystal floor clear and blazing,
Pillars of radiant gems alluring and
A canopy made brilliant with pearls.

Just as when Buddha took birth
The gods appeared and offered him water,
This bath of mystic water I now myself
Offer to this visualized assembly.
OM SARVA TATHAGATA ABHISHIKATA SAMAYA SHRI YE
AH HUM.

Although the body of a Buddha has no delusion;
In order to purify the physical obscurations of beings

I offer this water to the Buddhas' bodies.
May the physical obstructions of beings be cleansed.
OM SARVA TATHAGATA ABHISHIKATA SAMAYA SHRI YE AH HUM.

Although the speech of a Buddha is without impediment;
In order to purify the obstructions of beings' speech
I offer this water to the Buddhas' speech.
May the obstructions of being's speech be cleansed.
OM SARVA TATHAGATA ABHISHIKATA SAMAYA SHRI YE AH HUM.

Although the mind of a Buddha has no confusion;
In order to purify the mental obstructions of beings
I offer this water to the Buddhas' mind.
May the mental obstructions of the beings be purified.
OM SARVA TATHAGATA ABHISHIKATA SAMAYA SHRI YE AH HUM.

Although the three doors of a Buddha are without delusions;
In order to purify the stains of beings' three doors
I offer this water to the Buddhas' three doors.
May the stains of beings' three doors be cleansed.
OM SARVA TATHAGATA ABHISHIKATA SAMAYA SHRI YE AH HUM.

Now with unequalled fragrant cloth
I dry and polish their bodies.
OM HUM TRAM HRIH AH KAYA VISHODHANAYA YE SVAHA.

Although their form-aggregate by nature is pure
And is without chains of craving,
In order to purify ourselves of stains
We offer their bodies this mystic water.
OM SARVA TATHAGATA ABHISHIKATA SAMAYA SHRI YE AH HUM.

O Buddhas and Sons of Buddhas,
To the accompaniment of music and song

I offer to your holy bodies
Precious vases filled with perfumed oils.
OM SARVA TATHAGATA AHISHIKATA SAMAYA SHRI YE
AH HUM.

Sentient beings are suffering with thirsts of delusion.
In order to satiate them with waters of Dharma
And to free them from all faults
I offer this vase filled with water.
OM SARVA TATHAGATA AHISHIKATA SAMAYA SHRI YE
AH HUM.

This water is in nature generosity
Able to wash away the stains of my greed.
In this water beautifully scented with generosity
I invite you to bathe your bodies.
OM SARVA TATHAGATA AHISHIKATA SAMAYA SHRI YE
AH HUM.

This water is in nature ethical discipline
Able to wash away the stains of my moral corruption.
In this water beautifully scented with ethics
I invite you to bathe your bodies.
OM SARVA TATHAGATA AHISHIKATA SAMAYA SHRI YE
AH HUM.

This water is in nature patience
Able to wash away the stains of my anger.
In this water beautifully scented with love
I invite you to bathe your bodies.
OM SARVA TATHAGATA AHISHIKATA SAMAYA SHRI YE
AH HUM.

This water is in nature joyous perseverance
Able to wash away the stains of my lassitude.
In this water beautifully scented with energy
I invite you to bathe your bodies.
OM SARVA TATHAGATA AHISHIKATA SAMAYA SHRI YE
AH HUM.

This water is in nature meditative concentration
Able to wash away the stains of my mental wandering.
In this water beautifully scented with samadhi
I invite you to bathe your bodies.
OM SARVA TATHAGATA AHISHIKATA SAMAYA SHRI YE
AH HUM.

This water is in nature wisdom
Able to wash away the stains of my wisdom corruption,
In this water beautifully scented with wisdom
I invite you to bathe your bodies.
OM SARVA TATHAGATA AHISHIKATA SAMAYA SHRI YE
AH HUM.

Pray, accept this mystic bath peerless and supreme,
And with the waters of your unequalled compassion
And the waters of your wisdom and blessings
Bestow upon me accomplishments of all desired things.
OM SARVA TATHAGATA ABHISHIKATA SAMAYA SHRI YE
AH HUM.

Now with unequalled fragrant cloth
I dry and polish their bodies.
OM HUM TRAM HRIH AH KAYA VISHODHANAYA
SVAHA.

2. *Offering anointing oils, clothing, ornaments, etc.*

With supreme oils possessing a million fragrances
I anoint the bodies of the Buddhas,
Which are as radiant as polished gold
And blaze with a brilliant light.[5]

Then I offer them sweet-smelling garments
Adorned with the most sublime of colours—
Raiments fine, delicate and soft
Surpassing the clothing of men and gods.

And with a hundred supreme ornaments
I adorn the bodies of the great Buddha-Sons:
The always sublime Samantabhadra, wise Manjushri,
Compassionate Avalokiteshvara, and all the others.

Soft, fine and light cloth of the heavens
I offer to those possessing the unbreakable Vajra body.
With unbreakable faith I make this offering
So that I too may gain that vajra body.

In order to train my mind I offer
Precious cloth radiant as a rainbow,
The mere touch of which bestows bliss.
May I thus be adorned by the cloth of patience.

The Buddhas are adorned with the marks of perfection
And for ordinary ornaments have no need.
Yet for the sake of beings I offer them ornaments;
May all become adorned by signs of perfection.

The environment of compassion, the banner of renown
The canopy of samadhi, the clear light of knowledge
And every other worthy sign I now offer
So that all living beings may gain wisdom itself.

I offer a precious vase embellished with jewels
And filled with the various mystical substances;
That the stains of our karma and delusion may be cleansed
And that we may be immersed in the waters of bodhimind.

To the King of the Shakya Clan I offer
A crown made of the purest gold
Radiating golden lights into the ten directions
And sparkling with every sign of splendour.

May it cause the Doctrine to fill the ten directions
And cover the world in goodness and joy.
May it aid all beings to attain the state of ten powers,
The highest ornaments of gods and of men.

3. The offerings of two waters five enjoyments and music

Oceans of mystical water of the Buddhafields
Formed from offering substances of an ocean of Buddhas,
To the Buddhas, an ocean of perfections, and their retinues
I offer with an ocean of faith; pray, accept them.

Oceans of cooling water of the Buddhafields
Formed from offering substances of an ocean of Buddhas,
To the Buddhas, an ocean of perfections, and their retinues
I offer with an ocean of faith; pray, accept them.

Oceans of flowers of the Buddhafields
Formed from offering substances of an ocean of Buddhas,
To the Buddhas, an ocean of perfections, and their retinues
I offer with an ocean of faith; pray, accept them.

Oceans of incense of the Buddhafields
Formed from offering substances of an ocean of Buddhas,
To the Buddhas, an ocean of perfections, and their retinues
I offer with an ocean of faith; pray, accept them.

Oceans of light of the Buddhafields
Formed from offering substances of an ocean of Buddhas,
To the Buddhas, an ocean of perfections, and their retinues
I offer with an ocean of faith; pray, accept them.

Oceans of perfumed oil of the Buddhafields
Formed from offering substances of an ocean of Buddhas,
To the Buddhas, an ocean of perfections, and their retinues
I offer with an ocean of faith; pray, accept them.

Oceans of celestial food of the Buddhafields
Formed from offering substances of an ocean of Buddhas,
To the Buddhas, an ocean of perfections, and their retinues
I offer with an ocean of faith; pray, accept them.

Oceans of music of the Buddhafields
Formed from offering substances of an ocean of Buddhas,
To the Buddhas, an ocean of perfections, and their retinues
I offer with an ocean of faith; pray, accept them.

4. The five sensory offerings

To the Buddhas, fields of limitless merit,
I offer supreme forms manifest yet having no self-nature.
With mind fixed on inseparable appearances and emptiness
I make this offering; accept it with your mind of inseparable bliss.

To the Buddhas, fields of limitless merit,
I offer supreme sounds manifest yet having no self-nature.
With mind fixed on inseparable appearances and emptiness
I make this offering; accept it with your mind of inseparable bliss.

To the Buddhas, fields of limitless merit,
I offer supreme fragrances manifest yet having no self-nature.
With mind fixed on inseparable appearances and emptiness
I make this offering; accept it with your mind of inseparable bliss.

To the Buddhas, fields of limitless merit,
I offer supreme flavours manifest yet having no self-nature.
With mind fixed on inseparable appearances and emptiness
I make this offering; accept it with your mind of inseparable bliss.

To the Buddhas, fields of limitless merit,
I offer supreme sensations manifest yet having no self-nature.
With mind fixed on inseparable appearances and emptiness
I make this offering; accept it with your mind of inseparable bliss.

5. Offerings of the Seven Royal Possessions

The skillful ones completely fill the Field of Merit
With offerings of precious wheels;
In order to be given the desired accomplishments
They wisely make this daily offering.

The skillful ones completely fill the Field of Merit
With offerings of precious jewels;
In order to be given the desired accomplishments
They wisely make this daily offering.

The skillful ones completely fill the Field of Merit
With offerings of precious queens;
In order to be given the desired accomplishments
They wisely make this daily offering.

The skillful ones completely fill the Field of Merit
With offerings of precious ministers;
In order to be given the desired accomplishments
They wisely make this daily offering.

The skillful ones completely fill the Field of Merit
With offerings of precious elephants;
In order to be given the desired accomplishments
They wisely make this daily offering.

The skillful ones completely fill the Field of Merit
With offerings of precious horses;
In order to be given the desired accomplishments
They wisely make this daily offering.

The skillful ones completely fill the Field of Merit
With offerings of precious armies;
In order to be given the desired accomplishments
They wisely make this daily offering.

6. Offering the universe

OM VAJRA BHUMI AH HUM, I lay the powerful golden base; OM VAJRA REKHE AH HUM, circling outside, the iron fence; in the centre, the King of Mountains; in the east, the continent Lupakpo; in the south, Jambuling; in the west, Balangjo; in the north, Draminyan; off the east continent are the islands Lu and Lupak; off the south are Ngayab and Ngayab Zhan; off the west are Yodan and Lamchok Dro; off the north are Draminyan and Draminyan Kyida.

(Above this I place) the jewel mountain, the wish-yielding tree, the magical cow, the uncultivated harvest, the precious wheel, the precious jewel, the precious queen, the precious minister, the precious elephant, the precious horse, the precious general, the vase filled with a great treasure, and the goddesses of beauty, garlands, song, dance, flowers, incense, light and perfume. And I place the sun, the moon, a jewelled umbrella, the banner symbolizing total victory, and, at the centre, the best things of men and gods.

This I hold up and offer to all the holy Teachers—my kind Root Guru and all the Gurus of the Lineage—and to the incomparable King of the Shakya Clan—Buddha Shakyamuni—as well as to his entire retinue. For the sake of living beings compassionately accept it; and bestow your transforming powers.

The swirling offering water is an ocean of learning;
The flowers are the knowledges; the incense is ethics;
The offering lights are wisdom; the perfume is faith;
The food offering is the ambrosia of samadhi;
And the offering of sound is a hymn of praise.
My body is a temple well adorned
With an umbrella of compassion, a banner
Of sympathy and a pennant of wisdom.

At my heart is a lotus of eight petals
And seated stably there is Buddha, object of my spiritual
 inquiry.
With mind thus focused I make this request:
Teacher of living beings, be always pleased with me;
King of Dharma, be pleased with me.

For as long as my enlightenment is not won,
I dedicate myself and my possessions to you,
As well as all good deeds of past, present and future
For the benefit of all living beings.

O Possessor of the eye of omniscience,
Supreme seat of veneration,
Look upon me with compassion.

Accept these my humble offerings
And bestow your transforming powers.

This earth consecrated with flowers, incense and perfumes
And adorned with the King of Mountains, the four continents and the sun and moon
I offer to this field of Awakened Beings.
May all beings enjoy the pure sphere.
IDAM GURU RATNA MANDALAKAM NIRYATA YA MI.

7. Shantideva's offering[6]

In order to hold firm the precious bodhimind
I make these offerings to the Thus Gone Ones,
To the stainless jewel of holy Dharma, and to the Sons of the Buddhas—
The great oceans of spiritual qualities.

I offer them every fruit and flower that exists,
All the various types of healing medicines,
Whatever jewels there are in the world
And water clean and enchanting.

I offer them mountains of precious stones,
Beautiful gardens, calm and pleasant lands,
Green trees adorned with supreme flowers,
And bushes with branches rich with delicious fruits.

I offer them every sweet fragrance of heaven and earth,
Pleasing incense wish-granting trees, trees laden with gems,
Rich harvests produced without human cultivation
And all ornaments suitable to offer.

I offer them all unclaimed natural splendours
Found within the boundless limits of space—
Lakes and ponds adorned with lotus flowers
And made exquisite with the sweet singing of wild swans.

Fixing all these within my imagination,
I offer them to Buddha, supreme of men, and to his spiritual sons.

Compassionate dwelling places of every excellent quality,
Look on me with sympathy and accept these my meagre
gifts.

I, having few merits, am not wealthy,
And have no other offerings to make;
Therefore, O Lords intent on helping the world,
For my sake use your powers to accept these visualized things.

O Victorious Ones and your spiritual sons,
I offer you my bodies of all my lives.
O Fearless Lords, accept me
And permit me to be your humble subject.

Living under your constant care
I would be fearless and would benefit the world
I would transcend all past faults
And in future would create no more.

To the Able Ones, supreme sites of my devotion,
I offer lotuses, mandara blossoms,
And utpalas, all having exquisite fragrances
And arranged in beautiful garlands,

I offer them billowing clouds of incense
Having an all-pervading aroma to stir the mind;
And I offer them all foods of the gods
And every drink sweet to the lips.

I offer them jewelled lamps
Standing on golden lotus bases,
And an earth anointed with perfumed waters
And graced by scattered flower blossoms.

Inconceivable mansions ablaze with jewels
Made beautiful with every pleasing sound
And with ornaments boundless as space
I offer to those whose essence is compassion.

Opened umbrellas of exquisite shape
Having handles of the purest gold

And canopies bedecked with jewels
I constantly offer to the Able Ones.

In addition may this infinite mass of offerings
Accompanied by an ocean of alluring music
Abide as clouds throughout eternity
To soothe the misery of living beings.

May an unbroken stream of rain
Of offerings such as flowers and gems
Fall upon the monuments of Dharma—
The stupas, sacred images and so forth.

Just as Manjushri and the other Bodhisattvas
Made offerings to the Victorious Ones,
Likewise do I myself make offerings
To the Thus Gone Lords and their spiritual sons.

To the vast oceans of excellent qualities
I send forth an ocean of praise.
May it become a gigantic cloud
To fill the entirety of existence.

IV

Purification of Negativity

1. Contemplating Refuge, evil and death

To all the Buddhas of the past, present and future[7]
And to the Dharma and the Supreme Assembly
I prostrate, visualizing myself as having
Bodies numerous as the atoms of the Buddhafields.

I prostrate to the foundations of bodhimind
And to all the spiritual monuments,
As well as to the masters and learned sages
And to those well established in training.

Until the heart of bodhi is attained,
I turn to the Buddhas for refuge,
And also I turn to the holy Dharma
And to the assembly of Bodhisattvas.

With palms pressed together I call out
To the Buddhas and Bodhisattvas,
Who are Lords of Great Compassion
Abiding throughout the directions.

Circling in samsara since the beginningless time
I have created many negative deeds
In this and countless previous lives,
And have instigated multifold evils.

Pressed by crazy darkness and confusion
I took great joy in these misdeeds.
O masters, looking back upon my past,
The depths of my heart know regret.

Overpowered by delusion,
My body, speech and mind have greatly
Harmed the Three Supreme Jewels,
My teachers, parents and others.

Before the Leaders of the world I acknowledge
All the unbearable suffering I have created
Through the force of a mind governed
By faults and shortcomings alone.

But should I be struck down by Death
Before the stains of this evil are cleansed,
How will I avoid their effects?
Therefore immediately I seek refuge.

The unpredictable Lord of Death
Waits not for what is done or left undone.
Whether I am sick or not,
My fragile life is in constant peril.

I did not think that one day
I would have to leave all behind,
But for the sake of friends and others
Indulged in many negative deeds.

Yet my friends will become nothing,
Others will become nothing,
I will also become nothing,
And everything will become nothing.

Like the things known in a dream,
Whatever I now own or do
Will become merely objects of memory,
Having passed, it will never be seen again.

Even in this short life
Many friends and others have passed.
But any negative karma I made for them,
No matter how terrible, remains with me.

Not having understood
The transient nature of life,
Countless evils I created
Out of attachment, aversion and ignorance.

Without pausing day or night
My lifespan is constantly draining away
And nothing is being done to stop it.
How will the moment of my death not come?

When I lie upon my dying bed,
I alone will experience
The feelings of my life departing,
Although all friends and relatives surround me.

When the agents of Death seize me,
How can friends or relatives help?
At that moment only positive deeds can help,
But that is something I rarely sought.

O master, I, lacking awareness,
Thought not of this terror
And for this impermanent lifespan
Created many great evils.

Even an individual being led to a room
Where his limbs will be cut off
Becomes petrified: his mouth dries, eyes sink
And his manner completely changes.

How much more terrified is he
Seized by the horrific forms
Of the terrible Lord of Death
And struck by the disease of passing away?

Trembling and with staring eyes
I shall search the four directions for refuge:
"Who is able to save me
From this overwhelming terror?"

But finding nothing in the four directions,
My heart will sink in darkness.
If there is no refuge then,
What shall I be able to do?

Thus to Buddha, protector of the living
He who strives to save the world
And who by strength overcomes fear,
Today I turn for refuge.

And to the Dharma that he has internalised
And which disperses worldly terror—
And to the assembly of Bodhisattvas,
I likewise turn for refuge.

Quivering with fear I offer myself
To Samantabhadra, the 'Always Sublime Bodhisattva',
And to melodious Manjushri,
I offer my body.

With a plaintive cry I call
To Avalokiteshvara, the 'Bodhisattva of Compassion',
Whose mercifulways are unmistaken:
"O Sympathetic One, grant protection to this sinner."

To Arya Akashagabha, 'Essence of Space,'
Arya Ksitigarbha, 'Essence of Earth',
And all the other Lords of Compassion
I utter a heartfelt cry for refuge.

To Vajrapani, 'Holder of the Diamond Sceptre',
The mere sight of whom causes the Agents
Of Death to scatter into the four directions,
I bow and turn for refuge.

O Compassionate Bodhisattvas, previously
I abandoned your advice; but now,
Filled with fear, I turn to you for refuge.
Pray, quickly disperse my terror.

If one should follow a doctor's advice
When afflicted merely by an ordinary disease,
What need to say the importance of following the teachings
When struck with the disease of hundreds of delusions?

Merely one of these delusions
Has power to destroy the whole mankind on earth;
And, except for knowledge, a medicine able to cure these
delusions
Is not to be found in any direction.

Are not then the actions foolish
Which contradict the advice
Of the Omniscient Buddhas, who are doctors
Able to cure all ills?

One is careful when standing
Beside even a small cliff;
What should be said to those standing
Beside the cliff falling to hell?

It is not safe to sit complacent
Thinking that I will not die today,
For the time of my death
Will definitely come.

Who can give me fearlessness?
How can I be set free?
Since without doubt I will die,
How can my mind remain relaxed.

What now remains with me
Of all my past experiences?
Yet out of attachment to the transient
In the past I contradicted the Teacher's advice.

But what use are likes and dislikes
When I must leave all behind
And alone must wander
From this life to the next?

How can I become free
From the misery caused by evil?
Day and night I should constantly think
Of this one thing alone.

All that through ignorance and confusion
I have done in the past,
Such as the inexpressibly evil deeds
And the various forms of unwholesome actions,

In the presence of the Enlightened Ones
I acknowledge and confess,
Prostrating again and again, my palms joined,
My mind aware of the horror of evil.

O Guides and Leaders of the world,
Help me to purify the stains of my wrongs,
Because they are not wholesome
In future I will do them no more.

2. A Sutra to the Thirty-Five Buddhas: Confessing a Bodhisattva's Downfalls.[8]

I, whose name is ...., for all times go to my teachers for refuge, go to the Buddha for refuge, go to the Dharma for refuge, go to the Sangha for refuge.

To Him who is the Bhagawan, the Tathagata, the Arhant, the Fully Enlightened One: to Guru Shakyamuni Buddha I bow down. To the Tathagata Great Destroyer Destroying with Vajra Essence I bow down. To the Tathagata Jewel Radiating Light I bow down. To the Tathagata King Ruling the Naga Spirits I bow down. To the Tathagata Leader of the Warriors I bow down. To the Tathagata Supremely Blissful One I bow down. To the Tathagata Jewel Fire I bow down. To the Tathagata Jewel Moonlight I bow down. To the

Tathagata Whose Holy Sight Brings Accomplishments I bow down. To the Tathagata Jewel Moon I bow down. To the Tathagata Stainless One I bow down. To the Tathagata Glorious River I bow down. To the Tathagata Pure One I bow down. To the Tathagata Bestower of Purity I bow down. To the Tathagata Lord of Water I bow down. To the Tathagata Lord of Water Lords I bow down. To the Tathagata Glorious Goodness I bow down. To the Tathagata Glorious Sandalwood I bow down. To the Tathagata Unlimited Splendour I bow down. To the Tathagata Glorious Light I bow down. To the Tathagata Magnificent One Without Sorrow, I bow down. To the Tathagata Lord of the Desireless Ones I bow down. To the Tathagata Glorious Flower I bow down. To the Tathagata who understands reality by enjoying the Radiant Light of Purity I bow down. To the Tathagata who understands reality by enjoying the Radiant Light of the Lotus I bow down. To the Tathagata Glorious Wealth I bow down. To the Tathagata Glorious Mindful One I bow down. To the Tathagata Glorious One whose Mind is Extremely Renowned I bow down. To the Tathagata King Holding a Victorious Banner over the Senses I bow down. To the Tathagata Glorious One who Completely Subdues Everything I bow down. To the Tathagata Conqueror In All Battles I bow down. To the Tathagata Glorious One Gone Beyond to Perfect Self-Control I bow down. To the Tathagata Glorious One who Arranges Appearances for All I bow down. To the Tathagata Jewel Lotus who Subdues All I bow down. To the Tathagata, the Bhagawan, the Fully Enlightened One, the Great Jewel Always Remaining In the Lotus, The King with Power over Mountains, I bow down.

O all you thirty-five Buddhas, and others—as many as there are of Tathagatas, Arhants and Fully Enlightened Ones who are existing, sustaining and abiding in the nature of the three holy kayas: Buddhas and Bhagawans who live in all ten directions of the sentient beings' worlds, please give me your attention. In this life and from the endless beginning of life in samsara, in the life preceding this one and in all the samsaric realms of birth, I have created much negative karma, have encouraged others to do so, or have rejoiced in the creation of it. I have forcibly taken offerings to the reliquary, offerings to the Sangha, have stolen or taken by force material things belonging to the Sangha, have created the five extreme, negative actions as well as the five negative actions that are close to them, have encouraged others to create these actions, and have rejoiced in the creation of them. I have involved myself in the paths of the ten evil actions, encouraged others to get involved in them, or rejoiced in the creation of them. Now, obscured, I fear that these karmas may cause me and others to be reborn in the hells, as an animal, as a hungry ghost, or in irreligious countries, as a barbarian, as a long-life god, as a living being with imperfect organs, holding wrong views, or not being pleased with Buddha's coming.

All these negativities I now declare. I admit them to be negative. I will not keep them secret by not confessing. I will not hide them. From now on, I will cut off and abstain from creating these negative actions. In the presence of the Buddhas and Bhagawans who become the transcendental wisdom of knowing all existence; who become the compassionate eye looking at sentient beings all the time; who bewitness, as the omniscient mind sees exactly whatever negative and positive karmas are created; and who become true knowledge, as the Omniscient Mind fully seeing all existence and explaining exactly and without mistake to all followers: to you I make this confession.

O Buddhas and Bhagawans having transcendental wisdom knowing and looking with the compassionate eye, please pay attention to me.

In this and from the limitless beginning of life in samsara, in the life preceding this one and in all the samsaric realms of rebirth, whatever merits I have created by even small actions such as by giving just one mouthful of food to a being in the animal realm, whatever merits I have created by keeping precepts, and whatever merits I have created by following the conduct for receiving sublime nirvana, whatever merits I have created by fully ripening other beings' minds, whatever merits I have created by generating the bodhimind, and all the merits of the highest transcendental wisdom that I have created: all these above merits, putting together all my own virtues, and then heaping them together with those of all others, thus totalling all our merits, I will fully dedicate them to the highest, of which there is no higher, to that even above the highest, to the highest of the highest, to the Nirmanakaya which is higher than nirvana.

For this reason I will completely dedicate to the highest, fully accomplished enlightenment. Just as, the previous Buddhas and Bhagawans have dedicated, just as the as-of-yet undescended Buddhas and Bhagawans will dedicate, and just as the present Buddhas and Bhagawans are dedicating; like that, I also dedicate fully.

All the negative karma which results in suffering in the lower realms, I confess separately. I rejoice in all the merits. I persuade all the Buddhas to grant my request: May I receive the highest, most sublime transcendental wisdom.

To the sublime kings of the human beings: those who are living in the present time, those who have lived in the past, and those who have not yet descended, to all those who have knowledge as vast as an infinite ocean, with hands folded in the mudra of prostration, I go for Refuge.

V

Stabilizing the Bodhimind[9]

In the spiritual energy that relieves
The anguish of beings in misery and
Places depressed beings in eternal joy,
I lift up my heart and rejoice.

In the goodness producing enlightenment
I lift up my heart and rejoice.

I rejoice in the beings who have gained
Eternal liberation from suffering,
And I rejoice in those attained to Buddhahood
As well as in their offerings, the noble Bodhisattvas.

In the ocean-like virtue of the bodhimind
That brings joy to all beings
And in accomplishing the well-being of others,
I lift up my heart and rejoice.

To the Buddhas of the ten directions
I join my hands in respect.
Let blaze the light of Dharma's truth
For the beings lost in darkness.

To the Buddhas considering parinirvana
I join my hands and request

Do not abandon the beings in sorrow
But remain and teach for countless ages.

May any spiritual energy thus generated
By my devotion to the enlightened ones
Be dedicated to dispelling the misery
Of living beings without exception.

As along as diseases afflict living beings
May I be the doctor, the medicine
And also the nurse
Who restores them to health.

May I fall as a rain to increase
The harvests that must feed the living beings
And in ages of dire famine
May I myself serve as food and drink.

May I be an unending treasury
For those desperate and forlorn.
May I manifest as what they require
And wish to have near to them.

My body, every possession
And all goodness past, present and future
Without remorse I dedicate
To the well-being of the world.

Suffering is transcended by letting go everything
And the mind aspires to transcend suffering
As one day all must be given up,
Giving it to universal happiness is best.

My bodily powers I dedicate
To the well-being of all that lives.
Should anyone wish to kill, abuse or beat me,
The responsibility is purely their own.

Should anyone wish to ridicule me
And make me an object of jest and scorn,

Why should I possibly care
If I have dedicated myself to others?

Let them do as they wish with me,
So long as it does not harm them.
May no one who encounters me
Ever have an insignificant contact.

Regardless of whether those whom I meet
Respond to me with anger or lack of faith,
May the mere fact of our meeting
Contribute to the fulfilment of their wishes.

May the slander, harm
And all forms of abuse
That anyone should direct toward me
Act as a cause of their enlightenment.

May I be a protector of the helpless,
A guide to those travelling in the path,
A boat to those wishing to cross over;
Or a bridge or a raft.

May I be land for those requiring it,
A lamp for those in darkness,
May I be a home for the homeless,
And a servant to the world.

In order to fulfil the needs of beings
May I be as a magic gem,
An inexhaustible vase, a mystic spell,
A cure-all medicine and a wish-granting tree.

May I act as the mighty earth
Or like the free and open skies
To support and provide the space
Whereby I and all others may grow.

Until every being afflicted by pain
Has reached nirvana's shores,

May I serve only as a condition
That encourages progress and joy.

Just as all previous Buddhas
First gave rise to the precious bodhimind
And just as they then carefully followed
The stages of the Bodhisattva disciplines,

Likewise for the sake of living beings
Do I now myself generate the bodhimind,
And likewise will I myself train
In the disciplines of a Bodhisattva.
(Repeat these two verses three times.)

They who out of wisdom
Have seized the supreme bodhimind
In order to further enhance it
The mind is uplifted thus.

From today I will reap the fruit of life;
Having well won the state of man,
Today I am born in the Buddha-Family
And am now a child of the Buddhas.

Thus in future I should make every effort
To live in accord with the Bodhisattva ways,
And never should I act as would bring shame
To this noble, faultless family.

As a blind man fumbling in garbage
Happens to find a rare and precious gem,
Likewise have I discovered
The jewel of the precious bodhimind.

Thus was found this supreme ambrosia to dispel
The Lord of Death, destroyer of life;
An inexhaustible treasure able to cure
The poverty of all sentient beings.

It is the highest of medicines
To quell the ills of the living,

And it is a tree giving shade
To those wandering on the paths of life.

It is a strong and mighty bridge
By which beings can cross from misery,
And it is a moon to shine in the mind
To clear away the pains of delusion.

The bodhimind is a great radiant sun
To disperse the darkness of unknowing,
And it is the very essence of butters
Gained from churning the milks of Dharma.

For all guests on the roads of life
Who would wish to taste the very substance of joy,
Here is the actual seat of true happiness,
A veritable feast to satiate the world.

Thus today in the presence of all Awakened Ones
I invite every living being to this festival
Giving both immediate and lasting joy.
May the gods and all others rejoice.

VI

Various Eulogies of Buddha Shakyamuni

1. From the Mahayanasutra-alamkara[10]

Homage to he who brings goodness and joy
And gazes with sympathy upon all beings,
Thinking only of how to give them happiness
And how to free them from pain.

O Able One free from every obscuration,
You outshine all the world
With a wisdom encompassing all to be known.
To he whose mind is free I bow down.

You tame the infinite sentient beings
Made wild with delusions and obscurations.
Homage to he who destroys delusions
But regards the deluded with compassion.

Homage to he who answers all questions well
Even while fixed in meditation on voidness.
Spontaneous one, Passionless Lord, I sing this praise
To you whose mind is always without hindrance.

Homage to the excellent teacher
Whose wisdom never falters
And who taught with words and knowledge
The basis and substance of that to be known.

Having gone to perfection you know the Way
And wisely teach the world
The true nature of coming and going
And the blissful path of clear abiding.

Those with the fortune to have seen you
Knew a most supreme being.
Merely by beholding your exalted presence
Their minds were filled with clear faith.

Homage to you who found all powers—
Receiving, abiding, giving,
Emanation, complete transformation,
Samadhi and wisdom of the ultimate.

Homage to you who destroys the maras
That confuse the beings in points of Dharma—
Methods, refuge, purity and
The very foundations of the Mahayana path.

Homage to you beyond the harms
Of the Tirthika teachers and yogis
Who confuse the meaning of renunciation
And are veiled from the wisdom that benefits the world.

Homage to you who sits with a retinue
Who have abandoned all the gross taints,
And who can speak on all points of practice
With strength and certainty based on knowledge.

Homage to you with perfect understanding
Which rests in omniscient wisdom
Never moving even for a moment
Into inferior knowledge or sensation.

Your efforts to benefit living beings
Spontaneously arise with perfect timing.
To he who constantly manifests as needed,
To the Always Active One, I bow down.

Six times each day and night
You look upon the world
With active great compassion.
To you who thinks only of benefiting, I bow down.

Homage to you who with deeds, insight,
Wisdom and enlightened action
Manifests as a Guru even to the Sravaka Arhants
And to the Pratyekabuddhas as well.

Homage to you who cuts the doubts
Of the infinite sentient beings
By revealing the great enlightenment
Of the three perfect kayas.

Homage to you who understands without fabrication
The great Truth vast and profound,
Without grasping, without fault,
And without taint, abidance or motion.

B. In Praise of Buddha Shakyamuni.[11]

Homage to the Three Supreme Jewels.

Having gone beyond the world,
  you serve as a light to the world;
Working for the good of the world,
  your mind indeed is sublime.
Having attained supreme illumination,
  you have cleaned away all stains of delusions;
Homage to Buddha,
  illuminator of the world.

Delighted to give the supreme gift
  and possessing ten supreme powers,
You have transcended discipleship
  but trains disciples as befits them.
I bow down to Buddha, the transcendent One
  who is beyond training

And who is worshipped by
gods, men and nagas alike.

Having gained all signs of perfection
you work for countless beings.
Homage to you who is unmatched
by anyone in the three worlds,
And whose golden aura
stretches for a span in length
To encompass your mystic form embellished
with every mark of goodness.

Having crossed over to the other shore,
you inspire perfection in others,
And the myriads of harmful devils
you crush and turn away.
Skilled indeed is you in knowing
the ways and thoughts of others.
To you who destroys negativity and evil
again and again I bow down.

King of the great Arhants,
destroyer of the stains of obscuration,
He who abides in perfect ways,
discipline and ethics,
Supreme lord among lords,
stainless one free of taints,
To you, possessor of supreme compassion,
I bow down.

After crossing the four rivers of sorrow
you taught well the four noble truths.
Most beneficial are your ambrosial teachings
opening eyes of wisdom for all the world.
Your mind knows no partiality,
yet looks on all with love,
And those who heed your words
are quickly turned towards truth.
To you with every excellence
I humbly bow my head.

Like a song gentle and sweet
was the purity of your voice,
And like the chant of Brahma,
god of the gods;
For it was made perfect with
the sixty qualities of excellence.
To you who gently spoke the truth
I bow and bow again.

Oh, homage to you who opened up
the wondrous path of liberation
For sages of clear mind ready
to enter into freedom
Through realization of emptiness, signlessness,
the sphere above aspiration:
The profound middle view
difficult to fathom and know.

Wise indeed are they who rely
upon the doctrine of voidness,
And unwise are they who forever grasp
at extremes of is and is-not;
You taught that the results of action are just
ripening of fruits.
To you whose view is unclouded
I bow my head in homage.

You well taught that the infinite things that exist
are forever free,
Coming from nowhere and
going nowhere,
Unreal like a magician's creation
and like a mirage:
Homage to you who dwelt
within this wholesome knowledge.

The born and the unborn: both
are without true birth;
The produced and the destroyed:
neither is to be seen.

Homage to the conqueror of
abiding and non-abiding,
Who did abide in the very abode
where abides the deepest Dharma.

This very nature of thusness
you thus perfectly taught
As you dwelt unwaveringly in
knowledge of thusness itself.
Homage to you who equals
an unmoving mountain,
Whose body is a mountain,
a vajra, a victory banner.

3. Shankarapati's Hymn to Buddha the Supreme

Homage to all the Tathagatas

I have met neither Buddha nor Vishnu,
Nor have I met Brahma or Mahadeva;
But I have heard of their forms, power, deeds and thoughts,
And have deeply considered their qualities and faults.

Vishnu leads a huge army bearing clubs
And Mahadeva is adorned with a necklace of human skulls;
But Buddha walks unarmed and in peace.
What should we admire, violence or peace?

Vishnu destroyed the lineages of Duryodana and so forth,
Mahadeva is said to have destroyed the triple city,
Guha (Kartika) also killed the crane (his uncle) with an
attractive short spear.
But Buddha thinks only of how to benefit others.

"I will harm this, will protect that, and
I will slay this," say the gods in their scriptures.
But Buddha does not think 'friend' or 'enemy',
But works to help them achieve enlightenment and
higher rebirth.

The teachings of Vishnu encourage attachments,
And the actions of Mahadeva are like a mad man.
But the Tathagata has destroyed all his faults.
Analyse who is worthy as the great teacher.

Some have no compassion and advocate harming others,
Whereas another advocates protecting all that lives.
Who has attachment and who has none?
Need I say which is the worthy refuge?

Indra holds a diamond sceptre; Bali has a killing plough; Vishnu bears a cutting disc;
Kumara carries a spear; and Mahadeva with his deadly trident resides in charnel grounds.
They are childish, without compassion and wields weapons, and create only suffering and fear.
Who with any wisdom would bow their heads to they who strive only to destroy life?

But there is one who walks without a trident and keeps no concubine.
He has neither cutting disc, spear, plough nor deadly trident.
Free of delusion, he works only to benefit others.
To him, the unmatched sage, I turn for refuge.

Mahadeva, overwhelmed by attachment, shamelessly and aggressively owns wife.
Vishnu, out of extreme anger destroys what he has done and Guha murdered even his own relatives,
Parvati, with anger kills buffalo (demi-god), and Mamos eat human flesh and fat.
Vinayak, has strong obsession for intoxicants, the One with the Ten Powers (Buddha) does not have even a fraction of faults.

I am not Buddha's friend, nor enemy of the Tirthikas;
Nor have I seen either Buddha or the Tirthika gods;
But I have studied the scriptures and ways of both,
And the excellence of Buddha has stirred my faith.

The Tathagata is not my father, nor the Tirthikas my enemies,
The Tathagata did not offer me wealth, nor did the Tirthikas steal from me.
But the Tathagata alone thinks only of how to benefit the world,
And it is solely to an object free of all faults that I am able to open my heart.

Whoever is pleased to help, and who works solely for the world,
Whoever rids the world of suffering and brings joy,
Whoever knows reality as clearly as the palm of his hand:
It is to that unmatched seer that my faith goes.

Perhaps with understanding, perhaps with love,
Or perhaps merely with doubt or just infront of others,
But whoever pays homage to the moon-like Buddha
Attains celestial glory and joy.

The followers of Vishnu say that once their lord,
Wishing to mitigate the suffering of mankind,
Took birth as the Shakya Prince, and became Gotama the Monk, and then Lord Buddha;
Are they not foolish, then, not to heed his teachings?

Others say that once Vishnu, overpowered by attachment and anger, stole the jewels of the asuras
And then, by means of cunning and stealth, seized their lands.
At that time, Vishnu while not liberated, still foolish people worshipped him.
And Buddha was fully enlightened, but ignorant people worshipped him not.

Narayana once offered Vishnu this entire world
Weighed down with four oceans, yet suffering alone ensued;
But as a result of offering Buddha a just handful of clay,
A child was reborn as King Ashoka and came to rule whole India.

Again I say, I do not side with Buddha
And I do not dislike the Tirthikas;
But whoever's teachings are reasonable
That I can look to as my teacher and guide.
We have to judge for ourselves with eyes of reason
And see who is worthy, who is wise,
And whose ways are beneficial to sentient beings.
What sensible person would do otherwise?

Were they without fault
And in possession of every excellence,
I would take as my teacher
Even Brahma, Vishnu or Ishvara.

But only to he without fault,
He possessing boundless excellences
And having both an omniscient and all-compassionate mind
Can I turn in my heart for refuge.

May any small merit of my having written this text
Which is an ocean formed from a thousand rivers of praise
To he whose wide eyes are like opened lotuses
Be a delight to all who hear it.

VII

Recitation of the Buddha Shakyamuni Mantra

To the Transcendent One, He Thus Gone, the Destroyer of the foe Delusion, the perfectly and completely Awakened One,
The mighty conqueror Buddha Shakyamuni I bow down.
I make offerings and turn to him for refuge.
Pray, bestow upon me your transforming powers.

(*Now recite the mantra of Buddha Shakyamuni as many times as possible:*)

OM MUNI MUNI MAHA MUNI YE SVAHA

(*Then:*)

By the power of this practice,
May I quickly attain the state of Shakyamuni
And lead every living being
To that very state of wisdom and joy.

VIII

Various Prayers

1. The Vow of Universal Goodness[12]

In clarity of body, speech, and mind, I bow to all the Human Lions of the past, present, and future in every world in all the ten directions.

By the power of the vows of the deeds of goodness, I manifest in the mental presence of all the Victors in their lands as numerous as atoms and, prostrating all my bodies, I salute every one of those Victors.

As many Buddhas as there are atoms present in each atom, each sitting at the head of many Buddha-Sons; I believe that the entire Realm of Truth is filled up with all these Enlightened Ones.

I praise all these Blissful Lords, expressing their excellences as Victors with all the sounds of the ocean of words and melodies, oceans of their inexhaustible praises.

I worship those Conquerors with the best flowers, the best garlands, cleansing waters, ointments, superb perfumes, the finest lamps, and the best incense.

I worship them with all the superb and excellent arrays, the best robes, the best scents, incense powders piled up as high as Mount Meru.

I commit all those magnificent and unexcelled offerings equally to all the Victors; and by the power of my faith in the deeds of goodness, I salute and worship them.

I specifically confess all those sins, whichever I committed either physically, verbally, or mentally, under the influence of greed, hatred, and delusion.

I heartily congratulate all those beings for all their meritorious deeds, all the Buddhas of the ten directions, the Buddha-Sons, the Self-Enlightened Sages, the Learners and the Masters.

I exhort those lamps of the worlds of the ten directions, those protectors who have attained the detachment of Buddhahood in the stage of enlightenment—I urge them to turn the unexcelled Wheel (of Dharma).

To those Buddhas who enjoy manifesting final nirvana to gladden and benefit all living beings, with palms pressed together I beseech them to remain for as many aeons as there are atoms in all the Buddha-lands.

Whatever little virtue I may have gained from saluting, offering, confessing, rejoicing, exhorting, and beseeching, may all be dedicated to perfect enlightenment.

May I worship the Buddhas of the past and those now present in the worlds of the ten directions; and may those not yet arrived quickly fulfil their aspiration and reach Buddhahood at the seat of enlightenment.

May the vast array of all the lands of the ten directions all become pure! May they be filled with Victors who proceed to the royal tree of enlightenment and with the Buddha-Sons.

May all living beings whatsoever in the ten directions always be happy and free of sickness! May there always be harmony between the meanings of the religions of all beings! And may all achieve their hopes!

May I perform all the deeds of enlightenment and remember my lives in all states of existence! And after death, migration, and birth in all my lives, may I always renounce the world!

Becoming the disciple of all the Victors, fully accomplishing the deeds of goodness, pure in the immaculate deeds of morality, may my conduct always be flawless and without lapses.

May I teach the Dharma in every language, as many as there are words of living beings, in the languages of the gods, the nagas, the yakshas, the sprites, and the humans.

Gently, may I always strive in the transcendences, and may I never forget the spirit of enlightenment. Whatever sins may come to obstruct me, may I completely purify all of them!

Liberated from action, delusions, and evil deeds, in all the migrations of the worlds, just like a lotus unsplashed by the water, so may I proceed unhindered, like the sun and moon in the clear sky!

In all the lands in all the directions, may the sufferings of the hellish migrations be completely eradicated! Establishing beings in happiness, may I work for the benefit of all living beings!

Fully accomplishing the deeds of enlightenment, may I work in harmony with the deeds of all beings! May I work in all future aeons, showing the deeds of universal goodness!

Whoever's deeds are similar to mine, may I always associate with them! May our physical, verbal, and mental deeds always be unified, and may our vows be as one!

May those friends who wish to help me and always show good ways, always meet me again and again, and may I never renounce them!

May I always personally behold the Victors, those Guardians surrounded by the Buddha-Sons! And without tiring in all future aeons may I always make them magnificent offerings!

May I always uphold the holy Dharma of the Buddhas! May I always make shine the deeds of enlightenment! And practising the deeds of goodness, may I accomplish them in all future aeons!

Circling in all the states of existence, may I gather endless stores of merit and wisdom! May I become an inexhaustible treasury of all virtues of technique, wisdom, concentration, and freedom!

Those lands, of which there are as many in one atom as there are atoms, in each of which are inconceivable Buddhas sitting in the midst of their Buddha-sons; may I always behold them engaging in the deeds of enlightenment!

Thus may I completely enter into practice in every direction, in perfect awareness of the oceans of lands, oceans of Buddhas, and oceans of aeons of past, present and future being present in the space of each of the tips of my hairs!

The pure speech of the Victors contains within each statement an ocean of words and languages precisely suited to the interests of all beings; may they always engage with the Buddha Speech!

By the power of genius may I always get involved in the inexhaustible melodious speech when those Victors of past, present and future turn the various types of Wheels (of Dharma)!

May I enter all the future aeons even in a single instant! Even all those aeons past, present and future, may I practise entering them in a fraction of a second!

May I behold all the Human Lions of past, present, and future even in a single instant! May I always enter into their realms by the power of the illusory liberations!

Whatever lands are arrayed in past, present, and future, may they be achieved upon a single atom! And may I thus enter into the arrays of the lands of the Victors in all directions entirely!

May those Lamps of the Worlds who have not yet arrived manifest the sequence of Buddhahood, turning the Wheel, and the extreme peace of final nirvana; and may I always be in their presence.

May the powers of enlightenment be accomplished by the powers of magic of total swiftness, by the powers of the Universal Vehicle through every door, by the powers of deeds of every virtue, by the power of universally pervasive love, by the powers of merits of universal virtue, by the power of intuition which is unimpeded, and by the powers of wisdom, technique, and meditative concentration!

May the powers of action be utterly purified, the powers of passions be utterly vanquished, the powers of devils be utterly powerless, and the power of the Deeds of Goodness be utterly perfected!

May the ocean of lands be purified, the ocean of beings liberated, the ocean of Teachings understood, and the ocean of intuitive wisdoms fully realized! May the ocean of deeds be purified and the ocean of vows fulfilled. Worshipping the ocean of Buddhas, may my deeds be tireless throughout oceans of aeons!

Attaining Buddhahood through the deeds of goodness, may I totally fulfil all of the vows of deeds of enlightenment made by all the Victors of the past, present and future!

The name of the senior son of all Victors is Universal Goodness (Samantabhadra); I dedicate all these merits, that my deeds may have such skill as his!

May my body, speech, and mind, my deeds and my lands be always pure! And may I come to have just such skill as has that dedicated by Samantabhadra!

For the wholly virtuous deeds of goodness, may I also execute the vows of the Bodhisattva Manjushri, and tirelessly throughout all future aeons may I accomplish his duties!

May there be no limit to my deeds! And may there be no limit to their virtues! Persevering in such immeasurable deeds, may I attain all magical powers!

The limit of living beings is just like the limit of open space—may the limit of my vows be precisely the same as the limit of their actions and their passions!

I offer all lands of the ten directions, beautified with jewels, to the Holy Victors! I offer for as many aeons as there are atoms in those lands all the superb bliss of gods and men!

Whoever hears this king of dedications, may they gain intense aspiration for supreme enlightenment. Generating just once such faith, may they gain this supreme and holy merit!

Whoever makes this vow of Deeds of Goodness will abandon forever the hellish migrations, will abandon all evil friends, and will soon behold the boundless light!

They will obtain all benefits and live on happiness. They will come to this precious human life, and before long they will even become just like Samantabhadra himself.

Even those who out of ignorance committed the five unredeemable sins, if they recite this vow of Deeds of Goodness, will soon become completely purified!

They will come to have wisdom, beauty, the auspicious marks, noble birth, a good complexion. They will be untroubled by devils or escapists, and will be worshipped in all the three realms.

They will quickly proceed to the royal tree of enlightenment and will sit there in order to benefit all living beings; enlightened in Buddhahood, they will turn the Wheel of Dharma, and they will tame all the devils with their armies.

Whoever remembers, teaches, or even reads this Vow of Deeds of Universal Goodness, obtains the Buddha Wisdom as its evolutionary effect. May there be no doubt about the Supreme Enlightenment!

I dedicate all this virtue that I may learn from all those (great Bodhisattvas) becoming like heroic Manjushri in wisdom, and just like Samantabhadra himself!

From that dedication praised as supreme by all Victors of the past, present, and future, may I dedicate all these roots of virtue I have for the sake of the Deeds of Goodness!

When I face the moment of death, may all obscurations be cleared away, and directly beholding the boundless light, may I go to that blissful land of Sukhavati!

Reaching there, may all these vows become entirely realized! May I totally fulfil all of them, and benefit all beings in the universes!

Joyful there in that blessed assembly of the Buddhas, may I be born on an extremely beautiful, superb lotus, and may I personally receive the prediction of my own enlightenment from the Victor Amitabha himself!

There, having obtained that prediction, may I accomplish many benefits for living beings in all ten directions by the power of my genius with its hundreds of millions of magic incarnations!

Whatever slight virtue I may have gained from making this Vow of Deeds of Goodness, may it in a single instant fulfil all virtues of all vows of living beings!

By dedicating thus these vows of Universal Goodness, by whatever immeasurable holy merit is gained, may all those beings who are sinking in the great river of suffering actually attain the abode of Amitabha!

(May this supreme chief of Kings of Vows benefit all limitless beings! Completing the Scripture adorned by Samantabhadra, may it entirely empty all hellish migrations of beings!)

2. A Prayer Giving Rise to Enlightenment[13]

Homage to the youthful Manjugosha.

I bow down to the transcended and attained Buddha,
The blossomed lotus whose wisdom has cleared away the
darkness of wrong concepts,
Who, having destroyed the enemies called Four Maras, has
perfectly gone to Thusness,
And whose swirling lake of compassion is a treasure endowed
with supreme meaning.

I bow down to the pure and holy Dharmas
Which are signless as the sky, are free of false assertions, are
at peace,

Are free from faults of obscurations, are sources of every good quality,
And which turn the guest-like beings toward the path giving rise to bodhi.

I bow down to the exalted Sanghas,
Who, Victorious over the foe Delusion have forded the waters of becoming,
Have abandoned the tools of misery, have understood the path of perfect freedom,
And are places of excellent qualities working for the good of the world.

I bow down to the assembly of Bodhisattvas,
The sun of whose wisdom shines in the centre of the sky of dharmadhatu
To disperse darkness and give realization of pure truth;
Who, knowing every method and having all compassion, strive ceaselessly to benefit living beings.

To these treasures of good qualities and to those born from them
I offer a jewelled earth with wish-fulfilling gardens
Having an inconceivable mansion and throne adorned with precious jewels
All clothed in clouds of transcendental offerings.

Throughout countless lives I have turned my back on the Three Supreme Jewels,
Having claimed offerings made to them, have relinquished the enlightened attitude,
And have committed many shameful deeds, such as the in expiable actions.
In the presence of the Gurus I now acknowledge these and vow never to do them again.

And I rejoice in all the infinite goodness
Of the merits, both as cause and effect,
Of the Buddhas, Pratyekabuddhas, Sravaka Arhants,
Bodhisattvas, and ordinary beings as well.

O you who for the sake of living beings won enlightenment
And are now considering passing into final peace,
I entreat you, do not enter into parinirvana
But turn the holy Dharma-Wheels for the sake of the world.

O you free of faults and having every excellence—
O Buddha, Dharma and exalted Sangha—
At all times I offer myself to you and turn to you for refuge.
Pray, accept me; and protect me from misleading paths.

In order to clear away the delusions of beings
And in order to enact all the deeds of enlightenment,
O Knowers of All Time, you found peerless awakening
Which abides in neither samsara nor nirvana, and is beyond all projections.

Now I call to you: Buddhas and Bodhisattvas of the ten directions, gaze upon me,
And accept my pledge of practice:
From now until enlightenment is won I shall abide
In the three trainings—the moralities of restraining from wrong, producing goodness and benefiting others.

And by any merits of my thus practising,
May clouds of peerless offerings arise to please the Holy Ones.
May the obscurations of sentient beings be cleansed
And may their good qualities reach fulfilment, even until the state of omniscience is won.

May I myself always possess a mind of compassion
And by my gaining the supreme doors of samadhi, wisdom and retention,
May I place all beings in joy, enlightened conduct,
And the insight which understands things as they are.

May I assemble beings in the four skilful ways and complete the six perfections.
May I thoroughly train in the aspirational level and so on
And eliminate every delusion and obscuration hindering my attainment of exalted omniscience.

Thus may I complete the dual collection and reach Buddhahood itself.

May all beings merely by seeing, touching, hearing or remembering me,
Become pacified of every delusion and obscuration,
And may my body and mind become objects of virtue
Giving only happiness and joy to the world.

And just as the Buddhas of the three times have made dedications,
May any of the goodness and virtue thus produced
Throughout time by my body, speech and mind
Be dedicated to the peerless awakening of all beings.

3. A Selection from The Precious Garland[14]

To the Buddhas, the holy Dharma, the Sangha
And the assembly of Bodhisattvas
I bow and turn for refuge;
And I bow to all worthy of devotion.

Turning back the forces of evil
And holding firmly to goodness,
I rejoice in the mass of merits
Of all living beings.

With hands folded and head bowed
I call to the perfect Buddhas:
Pray, turn the Wheel of Dharma
For as long as sentient beings exist.

By the merits of my doing thus
And by what I have done or have yet to do,
May each and every sentient being
Gain the state of peerless awakening.

May the sentient beings have every pure power,
May they pass beyond all fetters,
May they have complete freedom of action
And may they live by excellent means.

May all the infinite living beings
Hold treasures in their hands;
And until samsara is exhausted
May they have everything needed.

At all times may all inferior beings
Aspire to higher states
And may all sentient beings
Have wisdom and wisdom's legs.

May they all have a life endowed
With good complexion,
A form radiant and sublime,
With beauty, health and strength.

May they be skilled in spiritual practice,
Free from the various forms of misery,
Devoted to the Three Supreme Jewels
And rich in treasures of the Buddhadharma.

May their ornaments be love, compassion,
Joy, equanimity in the face of delusion,
Generosity, discipline, patience,
Zeal, meditation and wisdom.

May they complete the collection of merit and wisdom
And manifest the major and minor marks of perfection.
Without hindrance may they transcend
The ten inconceivable Bodhisattva stages.

May I too be fully adorned
By these and all other excellent qualities,
May I become free from every fault
And abide in supreme love for all.

May I fulfil all the goodness
Aspired to by all living beings,
That I may be able to disperse
All the sorrows of the world.

May all the beings everywhere
Who are tormented by anxiety and fear
Be made completely and utterly intrepid
Merely by learning my name.

Merely by seeing or remembering me
Or by hearing the sound of my name,
May beings become joyful and unconfused
And gain the certainty of perfect enlightenment.

Throughout all their future lives
May they possess the five clairvoyances
And may I bring every benefit and happiness
To them all in every way.

May I always work to turn
Toward harmless states of peace and joy
All the countless living beings
Who enjoy evil and harming others.

Like earth, water, fire, wind,
Medicines and quiet forests,
Without resisting may I become an object
Giving joy to all sentient beings.

May others cherish me as they do their life,
And may I cherish them even more so;
May their negativities ripen upon me,
And my merits upon them.

For as long as there are living beings
Remaining unliberated in any realm,
May I continue to strive for them
Even though I had long attained enlightenment.

4. *An Aspiration in Seventy Stanzas*[15]

Homage to the Awakening Warrior:
The entirely good Samantabhadra.

Homage to the Buddhas Gone to Bliss
Endowed with an accumulation
of immeasurable precious qualities,
Who have uprooted every last poisoned tree
of moral failings
And who abide during the three times
throughout the ten directions.

Homage to the Truth of Dharma
That opens the wisdom-eye of beings
in all three realms,
That disperses the gloom of unknowing
And is the means for extracting
the poisonous arrow of latent tendencies.

Homage to the Sons of Those Gone to Bliss,
the Sangha intent on virtue
Who never revert (to worldliness)
And whose thoughts are motivated
by great compassion.
Unceasingly I bow my head to all
who have opened the eye of their mind.

Whatever slight non-virtue I have committed
throughout my lifetimes,
Or have encouraged, or rejoiced in,
I lay bare before the Conquerors
And pledge never to commit them again.

Without any exception I rejoice in the virtue
Accumulated by Those Gone to Bliss,
Solitary Realisers, Listeners and Conquerors' Sons,
And in other wholesome deeds of worldly beings.

Whatever non-virtue creatures commit
Confounded by venomous emotional afflictions,
For them may I surely plunge alone
With pleasure into the realms of hell.

Having satiated the world with the nectar of peaceful delight,

May everyone's mind become active in virtue.
May I willingly take on myself
As much misery as beings may have.

May perfect awakening itself be produced
Soon in the minds of these beings.
May those who have generated the pure awakening thought
Perfectly accomplish the collections for enlightenment.

By accomplishing the collections of virtue
  and attaining the spiritual levels,
By remaining in the lineage of Protectors of all
  three worlds,
And by annihilating the foes (of delusion),
May the abode of the Great Kingdom of Truth
  over the three worlds be attained.

No matter how many days there have been since
  the Awakened Beings
Became enlightened under the bodhi-tree,
I beseech those who are alive and abiding
Hereafter to cause the incomparable nectar of Truth to rain
  upon ongoing beings.

I entreat those noble-minded ones who have completed
Their sublime activities for the sake of others
And who are about to enter the supreme state beyond sorrow
To remain for a long time, acting to benefit others.

However many sentient beings there are
Wandering in the gloomy three worlds
I shall invite them as my guests
To savour the blissful nectar of extreme peace.

Whatever virtue has been accumulated in this way,
May it be dedicated totally for perfect awakening.
Thus may I never apart even for an instant
From bodhichitta—the mind intent on enlightenment.

Until the rank of those Gone to Bliss—
The basis of complete perfection—is gained,

May I never be apart from the leader
Of the Subduers and the Awakening Warriors.

They are the ones who finely elucidate
The path of activities for benefitting others.
May I also advance, free from despondency,
Through every spiritual level of the Sons of the Awakened Ones.

May my body be complete with the physical attributes of a human
And amassed with qualities worthy of praise by all creatures;
May I recollect past lives, be born to an honourable family
And have an attractive body.

Having discarded the vile action of ceasing to aid others
That zealously works for one's welfare alone,
(Aroused) by thoughts tormented with compassion
May I cherish dearly all creatures without favouring one.

May there be not the slightest grasping in the thoughts of others
At my possessions that I consider the wealth of others,
But may they take and use whatever they wish
Like someone who never doubts his own wealth.

Even if someone should demand my flesh,
May I offer it with pleasure in my eyes;
May I always donate my limbs and so on
For the welfare of all embodied beings.

May I, like a wish-fulfilling gem,
Provide all that beings desire
And may I, like the wish-granting tree,
Completely fulfil their hopes.

May I spontaneously banish
Evil actions far away like filth
And may I never breach the dam of precepts
Proclaimed by the supreme Subduer.

By abolishing concern for my body and life,
May I always enjoy places of solitude;
May my thoughts turn away from all gains
And honour as if they were poisoned food.

Like a child of lowly status, I will discard
Arrogance, self-importance and pride towards beings
And shall act to establish harmonious relations
As in a gathering of kin from a noble family.

May I be accustomed to ethical discipline,
An ornament utterly pacifying all (obscurations).
Stainless like moonlight and the root of a lotus,
Untorn, unmixed and unsoiled.

Even if someone against whom I have done no wrong
Should cut my head open, splitting it into hundreds of pieces,
I shall unceasingly hold him dear in my mind
Just as (a mother) cherishes an only son.

Should someone become angry with me from his heart
And needlessly rob me of my life,
May the unbearable and bitter fruits
Of his actions never arise.

Even if anger, abuse, provocation and aggression
Should besiege me, may I never forsake patience
But willingly take on all adversity
To practise the deeds of the Conquerors' Sons.

Thus, may the dangling rope of doubt
Never sway in my mind for even an instant
Over the extremely profound and highly logical
Dharma of the Subduer, that never before did I find.

May I who am born from lifetime to lifetime,
By earnestly acting to benefit all beings
Never fail to engage in vast virtues
For even a mere moment of time.

Like a servant, may I accomplish
All the tasks of every living being
And, having accepted the burden of working for all,
May sentient beings abide in happiness.

Since my body acts as a servant for others,
Even when speaking, may I be pleased to teach them Dharma,
And may even my thoughts constantly be empowered
By the mind endeavouring to benefit others.

Even if I alone have to undergo misery
For innumerable aeons in hell,
Still may I ripen sentient beings spiritually
Without ever becoming weary.

Surely, in the very process of accomplishing (the welfare of others)
I actually will put on this very armour
Of spiritually nurturing the three types of beings
So that they may become disciplined.

May I joyfully cross without hesitation
Pits so filled with burning embers of fire
That there is no space, so as to hear
Even one word of the good doctrine.

In abandoning being enticed by the results
Of all concentration and formless absorptions,
But by dwelling on the Supreme Limit of Perfection,
May I be accustomed purely to the bliss that arises.

Having mounted the horse of calm abiding
That is not obsessed (with the warm experience of meditative absorption),
May I tame the elephant of the mind
That naturally roams, is most difficult to tame and ventures along wrong paths.

Since the supremely fine riches possessed by
Rulers of Gods and Universal Emperors,

Being in the nature of desire are just like filth,
May I never hold them in high regard.

There is no joy drifting through this existence
Similar to a burning house of iron,
But, being led by compassion, may I be reborn
Wherever it is conducive to assist others.

Whatever absorptions all spiritual sons
Of Universal Protectors have mastered
Such as the Stance (of a Lion), the Inconceivable,
The Sport of a Hero, the Various Activities,

The Going Bravely, the Treasure of Space
And the Stainless, having attained all myself,
I will bestow their bliss on the three kinds of beings,
Thus allowing them to enjoy their sublime accomplishments.

May I thoroughly and supremely perfect
The ocean of craft, literature and art,
And may every sentient being be wise in knowing
The entire meaning of their own language.

Having gained the stainless, sharp and infinite
Intelligence distinguishing all words and meanings
May I share with sentient beings
The extremely profound and logical teachings.

To every living being without exception
Who does not perfectly understand Buddha's word
May I finely elucidate many teachings
As though inscribing letters on their minds.

Having surely ascended to the state of the ten fruitful powers
May I actualize those practices
That are the means for making the purpose
Of living beings completely worthwhile.

Just as all prayers of the Subduers
Are a cause for helping sentient beings,

So too may I work constantly
To attain the perfection of prayer.

By immediately suppressing as they arise
All overwhelming masses of foe-like emotional afflictions
And, not wavering from mental activities,
May I remain only to be of benefit on earth.

By having perfectly realised these phenomena
To be like illusions, mirages and magical emanations
And having discarded the mesh of conceptions
May I be of benefit throughout the three worlds.

Just as fathers especially cherish an only son,
So will I continuously remain in meditation
On pure love for every ongoing being
By removing all stains (of aggression).

Just as mothers out of affection for an ailing son,
In taking his burden on themselves, (suffer) accordingly,
So will I work to enhance my compassion
Towards each and every ongoing sentient being.

When I see success delighting others
May I, in especially generating much pleasure,
Remain meditating on joyfulness
As if my only dear son were happy.

Having dispensed with anger and attachment towards
  sentient beings
That correspondingly cause me to harm or to favour them,
May I accomplish the tasks of all three worlds
Like completing one's work for one's son.

Having realised the powers, clairvoyance, analytical
  knowledge,
Retention and the doors to liberation
May I simultaneously be of benefit to sentient beings
Throughout the immeasurable expanse of the universe.

Whatever countries where the name
Of "Buddha" has not entered the ear,
There may I act according to the deeds of Buddha
Through imparting his various methods.

Until the sun, the teacher of the three worlds,
Rises here in this universe, may I, like the sun,
Dispel the darkness (of ignorance)
From each and every embodied being.

Whatever beings there are whose thoughts are saturated with evil
And who have been rejected by many beings Gone to Bliss,
May they be tamed by relying upon
The sphere of action of my speech.

So that I may serve everyone in the universe
I will be loving like a relative,
Kind like a mother and, like a father,
Shall give beneficial advice.

Even by merely recollecting my name
May all beings immediately be
Protected from fear and may all misery
Of the three worlds be dispelled.

May I be a vase of goodness and medicine against illness
For people who are destitute in hundreds of ways.
May I also provide a cool pool of nectar
Continuously for the masses of hungry spirits.

May I be warmth for the cold hells and cause rain
With sweet breezes to shower on the hot.
As well, may I placate every harm
In the very low realms of bad migration.

Even by beings merely remembering me
May I be a true friend to those who face destitution,
Solid armour for those stricken by a rain of arrows,
And cooling water for those afflicted by fire.

When beings remember me may I be an opponent
For the venom of defilements, a firm bridge
Over the torrent of the three worlds,
And may I bar the door to unfortunate destinies.

May even merely recollecting my name be enough to prevent
All beings from falling into the abyss of worldly existence.
May I become the foundation of the stairway
Leading them to the pinnacle of pure peace.

Even if someone out of anger should recall
My name for just an instant of time,
May he never plunge into bad destinies
And may he surely accomplish perfect Buddhahood.

May my excellent qualities, stainless like moonlight,
Bring happiness throughout the whole universe;
May I work to generate immeasurable delight
For others even by merely breathing.

Having attained perfect awakening itself
Where all is fully complete
May I also settle all ongoing beings
In that ultimate awakening itself.

At that time, may not even slightly faulty actions
Arise in the minds of whoever (may be my disciples).
May they always help other creatures
And remain on the path of ten virtues.

May the realms of bad migrations never be seen
Even in dreams of anyone fitting (to be my disciple),
And may the far reaches of places of bad destiny
Be pleasurable like the realms of celestial beings.

As long as anyone remains in the midst
Of the ocean of the three worlds' non-virtues,
Though I have completed the deeds of a Buddha
May I remain in this world for them.

When I have enacted my passing into the State Beyond
Sorrow
May my teachings not become disordered
And may none of my followers be swayed
For even a moment by the dangling rope of doubt.

Thus, by delighting in the performance of the Conquerors'
Sons,
May whatever virtues I have gathered
All be shared by each and every
Living being without exception.

5. The Bodhisattva's Dedication[16]

Through the virtue of this effort to enter
Into the ways leading to enlightenment,
May all living beings
Come to engage in those conducts.

May all beings everywhere
Plagued with sufferings of body and mind
Obtain an ocean of happiness and joy
By virtue of my merits.

For as long as they remain in cyclic existence
May their (mundane) happiness never decline,
And may all of them uninterruptedly receive
Waves of joy from Bodhisattvas.

May all embodied creatures
Who throughout the universe
Experience hellish realms
Come to enjoy the bliss of Sukhavati.

May those feeble with cold find warmth,
And may those oppressed with heat be cooled
By the boundless waters that pour forth
From the great clouds of the Bodhisattva (merits).

May the forest of razor sharp leaves
Become a beautiful pleasure grove,
And may the trees of knives and swords
Grow into wish-fulfilling trees.

May the regions of hell become places of joy
With vast and fragrant lotus pools
Beautified with exquisite calls
Of wild ducks, geese and swans.

May the heaps of burning coals turn into heaps of jewels,
May the burning ground become a polished crystal floor,
And may the mountains of the crushing hells
Become a celestial palace of worship filled with Sugatas.

May the rains of lava, blazing stones and weapons
From now on become a rain of flowers,
And may all battling with weapons
From now on be a playful exchange of flowers.

By the force of my virtues, may those caught in the fiery torrents of acid,
Their flesh eaten away, revealing their lily-white bones,
Obtain the bodies of celestials,
And dwell with goddesses in gentle flowing rivers.

"Why are the henchmen of Yama, the unbearable buzzards and vultures afraid?

Through whose noble strength is joy brought upon us and darkness dispelled?"

Looking up, they behold in the firmament the radiant form of Vajrapani!

Through the force of their joy may they be free from evil and find his company.

When they see the lava fires of hell extinguished
By a rain of falling flowers mixed with scented water,
Immediately satiated, they wonder whose work this was:
In this way may those in hell behold Padmapani.

"Friends, don't be afraid but quickly gather here,
What need is there to flee when above us is the youthful
Manjugosha to dispel our fears,
The tender Bodhisattva who protects all living things,
Through whose might all suffering is removed and the force
of joy abounds

Behold him in an enchanting palace resounding with hymns
sung by a thousand goddesses,
With the tiaras of a hundred gods being offered to his lotus
feet,
And a rain of many flowers falling on his head, the eyes of
which are moist with kindness."
Upon seeing Manjugosha in this way, may those in hell cry
out loud with joy.

Likewise having seen, due to the roots of my wholesome
deeds,
The cool and sweet-smelling rain falling from joyful clouds
Created by the Bodhisattvas Samantabhadra and Sarva-nir-
vana-vishkambhi,
May all beings in hell be truly happy.

May all animals be free from the fear
Of being eaten by one another;
May the hungry ghosts be as happy
As the men of the Northern Continent.

May they be satisfied
By a stream of milk pouring from the hand
Of the noble lord Avalokiteshvara,
And by bathing in it may they always be cooled.

May the blind see forms,
May the deaf hear sounds
And just as it was with Mayadevi,
May pregnant women give birth without pain.

May the naked find clothing,
The hungry find food;

May the thirsty find water
And delicious drinks.

May the poor find wealth,
Those weak with sorrow find joy;
May the forlorn find new hope,
Constant happiness and prosperity.

May all who are sick and ill
Quickly be freed from their illness,
And may every disease in the world
Never occur again.

May the frightened cease to be afraid
And those bound be freed;
May the powerless find power,
And may people think of befriending one another.

May all travellers find happiness
Everywhere they go,
And without any effort may they accomplish
Whatever they set out to do.

May those who sail in ships and boats
Obtain whatever they wish for,
And having safely returned to the shore
May they joyfully reunite with their relatives.

May troubled wanderers who have lost their way
Meet with fellow travellers,
And without any fear of thieves and tigers
May their going be easy without any fatigue.

May those who find themselves in trackless, fearful
wildernesses—
The children, the aged, the unprotected,
Those stupefied and the insane—
Be guarded by beneficent celestial beings.

May beings be free from all states of no leisure
And be endowed with faith, wisdom and kindness;

With food (obtained in a proper manner) and excellent
  conduct,
May they be mindful throughout their lives.

May all beings be without want for wealth
Just like the treasury of space,
And without (it being the source of) dispute or harm
May they always enjoy it as they wish.

May those who have little splendour
Come to be endowed with majesty;
And may those whose bodies are worn with toil
Find magnificent and noble forms.

May all lower life-forms in the universe
Take (rebirth) in higher forms;
May the lowly obtain grandeur
And may the proud be humbled.

By the merits I (have accumulated),
May every single being
Abandon all forms of evil
And perpetually engage in virtue.

May they never be parted from the Awakening Mind
And may they always engage in the Bodhisattva's conduct;
May they be cared for by the Buddhas
And relinquish the actions of devils.

May sentient beings have lives
Inconceivably long (when in fortunate realms);
May they always live in contentment,
Unfamiliar with even the word 'death'.

May there abound in all directions
Gardens of wish-fulfilling trees
Filled with the sweet sound of Dharma
Proclaimed by the Buddhas and their Sons.

And may the land everywhere be pure,
Smooth and devoid of any rocks,

Level like the palm of the hand,
And the nature of lapis lazuli.

For all the circles of disciples,
May many Bodhisattvas
Dwell in every land
Adorning them with their excellent (manifestations).

May all embodied creatures
Uninterruptedly hear
The sound of Dharma issuing from birds and trees,
Beams of light and even space itself.

May they always meet with Buddhas
And their sons the Bodhisattvas,
Then may these spiritual masters of the world
Be worshipped with endless clouds of offerings.

May celestial beings bring timely rains
So that harvests may be bountiful.
May kings act in accordance with Dharma
And the people of the world always prosper.

May all medicines be effective
And the repeating of mantras successful;
May dakinis, cannibals and the like
Be endowed with compassionate minds.

May no living creature ever suffer,
Commit evil or ever fall ill:
May no one be afraid or belittled,
Or their minds ever be depressed.

In all temples and monasteries
May reading and recitation flourish and remain;
May the Sangha always be in harmony
And may their purposes be accomplished.

May monks desiring to practise
Find quiet and solitary places,

And through having abandoned all wandering thoughts
May they meditate with flexible minds.

May nuns be materially sufficient,
Abandon quarrelling (with each other) and be unharmed,
Similarly may all ordained ones
Never let their disciplines weaken.

Having repented any moral falls
May evil always be eradicated,
And thereby obtaining a happy state of birth
May spiritual conduct not decline even there.

May the wise be honoured
And may they receive alms;
May their minds be completely pure
And may they be renowned in all directions.

May beings not experience the misery of lower realms
And may they never know any hardships;
With a physical form superior to the gods
May they swiftly attain Buddhahood.

May sentient beings again and again
Make offerings to all the Buddhas,
And may they constantly be joyful
With the inconceivable bliss of the Buddhas.

Just as they have intended
May the Bodhisattvas fulfil the welfare of the world,
And may all sentient beings receive
Whatever the Buddhas have intended for them.

Similarly may the Pratyeka buddhas
And the Sravakas find happiness.

And until I reach the level of the Joyous One
Through the kindness of Manjughosha,
May I be mindful throughout my lives
And always obtain ordination.

May I live and be sustained
By simple, common foods,
And in all my lives may I find
The ideal solitude (for practising Dharma).

Whenever I wish to see something
Or even wish to ask the slightest question,
May I behold without any hindrance
The Bodhisattva of Wisdom himself.

In order to fulfil the needs
Of beings who reach unto the ends of space,
May my way of life
Be just like that of Manjughosha.

For as long as space endures
And for as long as living beings remain,
Until then may I too abide
To dispel the misery of the world.

May all the pains of living creatures
Ripen (solely) upon myself,
And through the might of the Bodhisattva Sangha
May all beings experience happiness.

May the teachings, which are the sole medicine for suffering
And the origin of every joy,
Be materially supported and honoured
And abide for a very long time.

I prostrate to Manjughosha
Through whose kindness wholesome minds ensue,
And I prostrate to my spiritual masters
Through whose kindness I develop.

(Note: If you do not have time to recite the previous two prayers, then recite whichever of the two that you prefer).

6. Prayer for the Doctrine to Flourish for Long[17]

Perhaps in a past life to benefit beings
I made great efforts in difficult practices
And sacrificed even my own happiness for them.
If so, may this cause the doctrine to flourish for long.

Perhaps in a past life to benefit the sick
I dedicated even necessities of life
To protect living beings from weakness and sorrow.
If so, may this cause the doctrine to flourish for long.

Perhaps in a past life to accomplish enlightenment
I renounced sons, daughters, wives,
Wealth, elephants and chariots.
If so, may this cause the doctrine to flourish for long.

Perhaps I once made auspicious offerings
To the Fully Awakened Buddhas, the Pratyekabuddhas,
Shravaka Arhants or my elders.
If so, may this cause the doctrine to flourish for long.

Perhaps in the past for countless aeons
I underwent endless hardships and trials
In the search for the meaning of true enlightenment.
If so, may this cause the doctrine to flourish for long.

Perhaps I once practised discipline and penance,
Applied myself to the austere yogas,
Or devoted myself to a Buddha of the ten directions.
If so, may this cause the doctrine to flourish for long.

Perhaps I once exerted great perseverance
And through constance in practice overcame a fault.
If so, may this cause the doctrine to flourish for long,
That countless living beings may attained freedom.

Perhaps I once showed strength in patience
And practised forbearance when heavily pressed

By the beings made cruel in this degenerate age.
If so, may this cause the doctrine to flourish for long.

Perhaps I once practised profound meditation
On the essence of some formless absorption
Or gained some of the millions of samadhis.
If so, may this cause the doctrine to flourish for long.

Perhaps in a previous lifetime to gain wisdom
I retired to the forests and practised intensely;
And perhaps I even expounded the healing Dharma.
If so, may this cause the doctrine to flourish for long.

Perhaps out of compassion I once sacrificed
May flesh and blood, or even my life;
Or perhaps I gave away the limbs of my body.
If so, may this cause the Dharmic ways to thrive.

Perhaps toward sentient beings evil and cruel
I practised love and thus ripened their minds,
And turned them toward one of the Three Vehicles.
If so, may this cause the supreme gift of Dharma to thrive.

Perhaps by the four ways of benefitting living beings
I freed some from the fires of conflicting emotions
And destroyed evil thoughts from within others.
If so, may I and those around me live for long.

Perhaps in a previous life I freed a Tirthika
From the chaotic waters of his wrong views
And placed him within clear understanding.
If so, may I and those around me gain renown
And may the sublime doctrine shine for long.

IX
Verses of Auspiciousness

1. Auspicious Verses on the Twelve Acts of Buddha[18]

Like a golden mountain having every perfection
Is the protector of the three worlds, He free of the Three
  Stains,
The Buddha with eyes like blossoming lotuses.
He is the first auspicious sign, bringing peace to beings.

The sacred Dharma, taught by the Unmoving Master,
Who is praised in the three worlds by both men and gods,
Brings eternal peace to living beings,
It is the second auspicious sign in this world of goodness.

The holy Sangha, rich with the auspiciousness of having heard
  the Dharma,
Are objects of worship of gods, men and spirits,
A supreme assembly of wondrous knowledge and glory.
They are the third auspicious sign of goodness in this world.

In order to benefit beings, the Lord of Enlightenment
Released great energy to accomplish the world's needs,
And opened up the path accumulating merit and wisdom.
By this auspicious sign, may all beings attain to peace.

In order to benefit beings the great Tathagata
Came to earth from the heart of Tushita's palace
Surrounded by an entourage of gods making him offerings.
By this auspicious sign, may all beings attain peace.

Then in Lumbini Gardens lavish with trees and flowers
He took birth with many gods as his support.
Thus appeared He Gone to the End of the World.
By this auspicious sign, may all beings attain peace.

The gods sang out in exuberant praise:
'Ah, Kapilavastu indeed is a holy city;'
And thus there arose an inconceivable mountain of goodness and joy.
By this auspicious sign, may all beings attain peace.

But the Prince was not content with royal life
And one midnight, aided by the gods,
Escaped to the forests to practise austere yogas.
By this auspicious sign, may all beings attain peace.

He with a golden body blazing with lights
Then prepared himself a seat with grass blue as lapis lazuli
And sat in the vajra-posture unmoving and still.
By this auspicious sign, may all beings attain peace.

Encircled by grass and trees on the banks
Of the Nairanjana River sat the wondrous destroyer of attachment,
And even the King of Nagas paid him tribute.
By this auspicious sign, may all beings attain peace.

Then he proceeded to the King of Trees, and through love
Tamed the vicious armies of Mara.
Countless transcendental omens appeared in the sky.
By this auspicious sign, may all beings attain peace.

To conquer misery completely, he remained in Vajrasana
And at dawn of the full moon quelled the four great maras,
Giving birth to the splendour of a Tathagata and Teacher.
By this auspicious sign, may all beings attain peace.

To Varanasi walked this supreme rishi,
Where he turned the holy Wheel of Dharma
And filled heaven and earth with wondrous omens.
By this auspicious sign, may all beings attain peace.

'These omens of good fortune herald great benefits
And infinite goodness,' cried out the beholders;
And the Able One, the Lion Amongst Men, spoke the magnificent Dharma.
By this auspicious sign, may all beings attain peace.

Then in order to benefit living beings he crushed
The pride of the Tirthikas by revealing magical deeds,
And thus became known as King of all Teachers.
By this auspicious sign, may all beings attain peace.

To uplift the world he travelled to the heavens
And returned again, accompanied by Brahma and the others,
Who were surrounding him and paying him homage by shading him with umbrellas and cooling him with fans.
By this auspicious sign, may all beings attain peace.

Finally the time came for him to enter into peace,
And countless gods appeared, sang his praises,
And offered him endless clouds of mandara flowers,
By this auspicious sign, may all beings attain peace.

The kings of gods, nagas and men bowed their heads in sorrow,
And the garudas, yakhas and gandharvas made offerings.
Thus passed away the Tathagata who possessed the ten powers.
By this auspicious sign, may all beings attain peace.

2. *Auspicious Verses on the Seven Past Buddhas*[19]

O transcended Vipashyi, All-Seeing One of the royal caste possessing a special radiance,
Who, when the human lifespan was 80,000 years in length, took birth in the city called Beautiful

And attained Buddhahood under the sharashali tree:
May the auspicious signs of your deeds manifest here now.

O blissfully gone Possessor of the Ushnisha, magical one of the royal caste
Who, when the human lifespan was 70,000 years in length, took birth in the city of Suba
And attained Buddhahood under the sundha tree:
May the auspicious signs of your deeds manifest here now.

O Conqueror Protecting All, wise one of the royal caste
Who, when the human lifespan was 60,000 years in length, took birth in the city called Incomparable
And attained Buddhahood under the sala tree:
May the auspicious signs of your deeds manifest here now.

O sage Kraukuchanda, transcended one of the Brahmin caste
Who, when the human lifespan was 40,000 years in length, took birth in the city called Blissful
And attained Buddhahood under the sharashali tree:
May the auspicious signs of your deeds manifest here now.

O leader and guide Kanakamuni, supremely disciplined one of the Brahmin caste
Who, when the human lifespan was 30,000 years in length, took birth in the city called Blissful
And attained Buddhahood under the udumwara tree:
May the auspicious signs of your deeds manifest here now.

O protector Kashyapa Buddha, one with peerless qualities of the royal caste,
Who, when the human lifespan was 20,000 years in length, took birth in the city of Varanasi
And attained Buddhahood under the nyagrodha tree:
May the auspicious signs of your deeds manifest here now.

O Lord of Living Beings, Buddha Shakyamuni, persevering one of the royal caste
Who, when the human lifespan was 100 years in length, took birth in the city of Kapilavastu

And attained Buddhahood under the ashvattha tree:
May the auspicious signs of your deeds manifest here now.

May the fortunate omens of these Seven Past Buddhas,
The wondrous blessings of the Sugatas of all times and realms
And the unfailing strength of the Dharmadhatu and of interdependent arising
Manifest now in this very place as an infinite mass
Of auspicious signs of the Mighty Ones Gone to Bliss.

Note: You can alternately recite one of the above two "Auspicious Prayers."

Notes

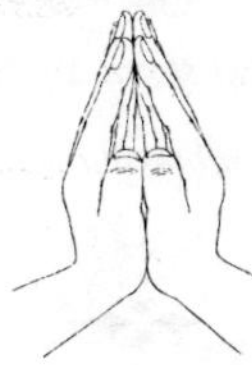

1. These opening verses are common to all Tibetan sects and are drawn mostly from the ritualistic works of Nagarjuna.

2. These are the opening verses of Nagarjuna's *Madhyamaka-Shastra*. The next verse that follows it are from Maitreya's *Abhisamaya-alamkara*.

3. This is a well-known Sutra passage in which a disciple of Buddha calls to him for inspiration. The Sutra states that after the disciple called out the above verses the Lord Buddha together with 500 of his monks transformed themselves into swans and flew to her, alighting on her roof and then changing back to their ordinary form.

4. Most of these verses come from Shantideva's *Bodhisattvacharya-avatara*, Chapter II.

5. Ibid., Chapter II.

6. Ibid., Chapter II.

7. Ibid., Chapter II.

8. This prayer of confession, known as *Tung-shak* (sTung-bShags) in Tibetan, is quoted in full in Shantideva's *Shiksha-samuccaya*, which is also a source of many of the offering verses above.

9. The *Bodhisattva-charya-avatara,* Chapter III.

10. These are verses from Maitreya Asanga's *Mahayana-sutra-alamkara*.

11. The *Bhagavan-Shakyamuni Stotra* by Acharya Triratnadasa.

12. Skt. *Arya-bhadra-charya-pranidana*, or "A Prayer of Noble and Sublime Ways", a very early Indian prayer. Five commentaries to this small work are found in the *Tanjur*, including one by Nagarjuna and another by Dignaga.

13. The *Bodhi-akara-pranidana* by Acharya Nagarjuna.
14. Nargarjuna's *Ratnavali*, Chapter V.
15. The *Pranidana-saptatinama-gatha* by Pandita Aryasura, otherwise known as Ashvagosha.
16. Shantideva's *Bodhisattva-charya-avatara*, Chapter X.
17. Tib., *bsTan-pa-'Bar-bai-smon-lam.*
18. The *Dvadashakara-nama-naya-stotra*, by Nagarjuna.
19. Nagarjuna's *Buddha-kamala-sabta-mangala-gata.*